TITANIC

A POSTAL COLLECTION

The remarkable history and legend as told through an extraordinary postal collection

▲ A pair of opera or field glasses found on the ocean floor near the titanic wreck.

▲ Mail sacks are loaded aboard Titanic.

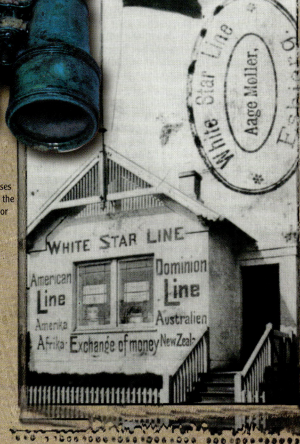

◀ A Postcard mailed from the Titanic with a postmark from Queenstown, Ireland on April 13, 1912

▲ Many Scandinavians were on the passenger list.

▼ Mailbags are prepared after the ship has boarded.

◀ The first and only 'Titanic Special' train heads toward Southampton for the maiden voyage.

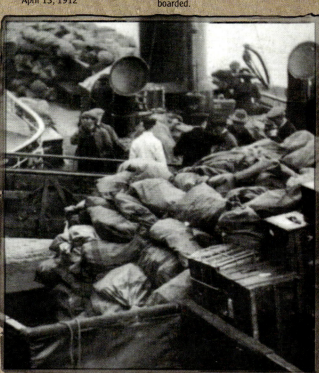

TITANIC
A POSTAL COLLECTION

Ever since word of the RMS Titanic's tragic demise on a cold April night in 1912, the legend of this 'unsinkable' luxury Trans-Atlantic liner has grown into mythology. Immortalized in print, song, on screen and even the Broadway stage, the story of this White Star Line steam ship and the loss of more than 1,500 passengers remains one of the great Maritime disasters in history.

The floating palace which began construction in 1907 was completed in 1912 and was considered the most luxurious ocean liner afloat. It began its maiden voyage from Southampton, England on April 10, 1912, complete with a first class lounge, a smoking room, grand staircase, Turkish bath, gymnasium, swimming pool and Squash court. At the time, the Titanic was the largest man-made moveable object in the world.

Overall 2,228 people were on board the great ship when it departed Queenstown, the last port of call before New York. This included 1,343 passengers and 885 crewmembers. In the end, only 705 persons would again see dry land, following the disaster on the night of April 14th, 1912. Due to the many circumstances for which the disaster could have been avoided and the extraordinary nature of the ship itself, Titanic has remained afloat in the consciousness of people and historians worldwide.

THE TITANIC POSTAL CONNECTION

Throughout the history of postage stamps, nations of the world have issued legal tender featuring topics and events that have shaped our world. Stamp collecting has always been a hobby for royalty and Presidents, but later became a teaching tool for children to learn about history, geography and international currency.

The impact of the Titanic tragedy was surely felt on both sides of the Atlantic where its passengers originated. Also, due to its magnitude and massive loss of life, the story has been retold countless times in books, film and song. Until recently, very few stamps or coins have been issued on the Titanic and most of them give little insight into its voyage, crew, design or luxurious nature. Issuing countries included Yugoslavia, Barbados, St. Vincent and Guyana. This unique postal collection from the nation of Madagascar should provide us with all of these elements and more.

Beyond its historical importance, the Titanic also had many postal connections that make it a highly appropriate topic for philately. Just the name alone RMS (Royal Mail Steamer) Titanic tells you all you need you know about its postal origins. Beyond this we have the following:

The least known but perhaps most important flag displayed by Titanic was her Royal Mail Pennant. This flag was only displayed by those vessels engaged in carrying His Majesty's Mail. It also confirmed the privileged designation "Royal Mail Steamer". This designation entitled Titanic to certain privileges at sea, and had Titanic made port, it would have been given preferential treatment as well. In this era, before cell phones, fax machines and when even the telegraph was a novelty, the display of this RMS flag was coveted by shipping houses and served as a symbol of great prestige.

Due to the industrious time that was 1912, the Titanic did include a busy post office. The Mail hold area was one of the first to fill up with water upon impact. The mail clerks tried desperately to salvage the sorted mail on the racks and the 3,420 sacks of mail, but they began to float away as the ship took on more water. On board the Titanic were five Royal Mail postal workers who were charged with sorting responsibilities and the safe delivery of the assorted letters, postcards and packages heading trans-Atlantic. It should be noted that because they remained at their duty stations, all five of Titanic's Postal Clerks perished. In Southampton, England a Bronze Memorial Plaque has been cast from the ship's spare propeller to honor the postal workers who were lost

Ironically one Postal clerk, William Logan Gwinn of Brooklyn, New York had been scheduled to work on another ship, the Philadelphia, but had received word that his wife was ill and requested to be assigned to an earlier voyage so he could get back home to her. Sadly he was transferred to the Titanic. Gwinn was lost when the ship went down, his body was not recovered.

Recently discovered card dated April 10, 1912 was offered at a Sotheby's stamp auction in London and had apparently been carried on the Titanic from Southampton. It was written by Robert Baleman, one of the eventual victims to his wife Ada who managed to survive on a lifeboat. The card displays the White Star Line flag and contained a British 1-Penny stamp of George V which is cancelled with a mark 'Transatlantic Post office/Ap 10/12.

The smallest property claim against the owners of Titanic came from the United States Postal Service totaling $41.04 for lost mail.

▲ Titanic at sail on the ill fated maiden voyage.

▼ The anchor of the Titanic is raised for departure.

▼ This telephone used for internal communication on the ship, was found in 1987

◄ A brass bell found amongst the wreckage.

▼ A view of the floating palace from the stern side.

▲ The ship is decorated with flags for the first and only time.

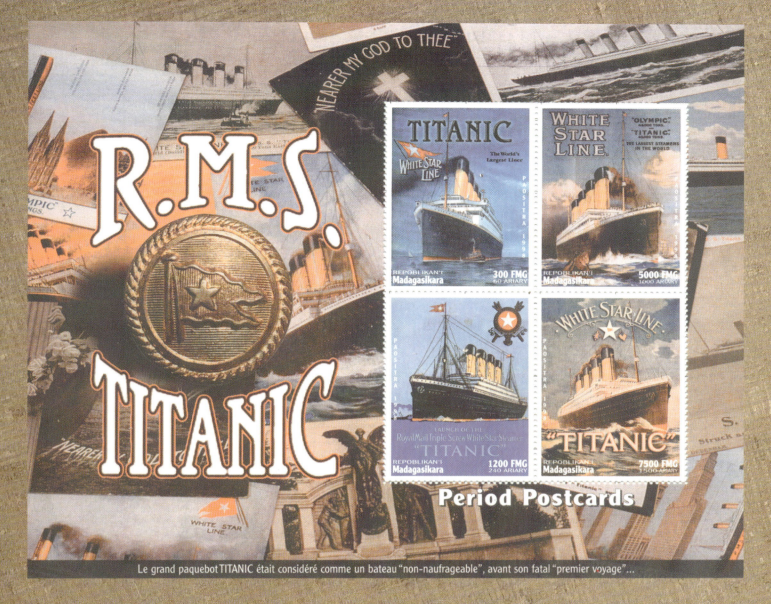

Le grand paquebot TITANIC était considéré comme un bateau "non-naufrageable", avant son fatal "premier voyage"...

THE GRAND TITANIC CRUISE LINER WAS CONSIDERED AN UNSINKABLE SHIP BEFORE ITS FATEFUL MAIDEN VOYAGE.

In the era of the Titanic, postcards were popular collectibles and keepsakes of one's trip to foreign destinations. Because of the remarkable glamour of the ships run by White Star Line, several of these postcards were created depicting the Titanic and the Olympic. The card's also were used to attract new business as noted by the impressive tag lines such as "The World's Largest Liner". It is likely that many of these cards were addressed and mailed on the Titanic's maiden voyage by its passengers. Like the ship, the mail never reached its destination. It is not surprising that the Titanic was so popular and glamourized in its time. The 'Ship of Dreams' was lavishly decorated and built over five years with the utmost care and expense. Although White Star Line never used the word 'unsinkable' to describe the Titanic, few if any ever imagined such powerful and state-of-the-art ship going down. Even more improbable was that Titanic would be sunk as a result of an iceberg in the cold Atlantic. But ironically this would be the fate of the most spectacular liner of its day. Also pictured on the above stamp sheet is the sheet music to the song Nearer My God To Thee which is thought to be the last song played by the Titanic musicians before the boat went under. It can be verified that the song was indeed one listed in the White Star Line songbook and survivors did recall hearing it as the boat was going down. However it can not be known for sure if this was indeed the last song played due to conflicting reports offered by those survivors who remembered the Ship's final moments.

▲ Construction of deepwater docks in Southampton.

▶ A triple toned whistle from Titanic was recovered in 1993.

▼ One of the three bronze propellers on Titanic.

▲ Here is the hull of Titanic being built.

▶ In 1987 the ship's telegraph was recovered.

▼ It took 20 horses to pull one of Titanic's 3 anchors.

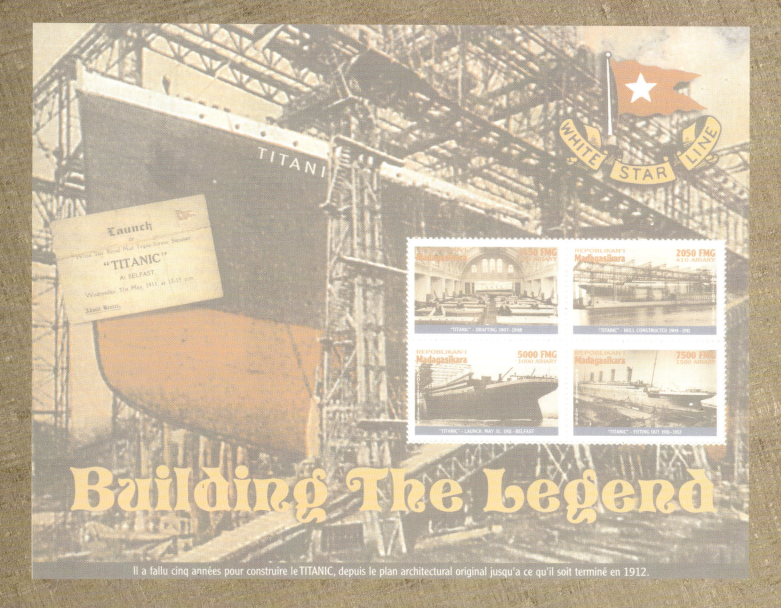

Il a fallu cinq années pour construire le TITANIC, depuis le plan architectural original jusqu'a ce qu'il soit terminé en 1912.

It took nearly five years for the Titanic to be built, from the original architectural draft until completion in 1912.

Built along with White Star Line's near identical ship the Olympic in Belfast, the two luxury liners cost a staggering 36 million sterling pounds. In 1912 this price would be considered steep, but today this amount wouldn't even pay for one. If the Titanic were built alone today it is estimated that the ship would cost more than $400 million dollars. Due to its luxury and majesty, the interior of the Titanic would be similar to furnishing a world class hotel. Crystal chandeliers, sculptures, spiral staircases and more would add up quickly in recreating such an extravagant structure today. It began as a dream in 1907 and took five years to build including the drafting by the Harland & Wolff company. While both the Titanic and the Olympic were built side by side, the Olympic would be launched first in 1910. Still the Titanic would be considered more luxurious and slightly larger. Nearly 15,000 yard workers were employed to build the luxury liner. Upon completion and fully loaded the Titanic weighed 46,000 gross tons and had the capacity to carry more than 3,400 passengers. The length was 883 feet and the width was 93 feet at its widest part. The draught or depth at which the vessel was measured was 34 feet. The ship's displacement was 66,000 tons of water. The Olympic was actually 1,004 tons lighter than Titanic. The primary reason as to why the ship was termed unsinkable was due to its 16 watertight compartments that insulated the interior. The Titanic was not considered to be the fastest Trans-Atlantic liner, but it was hardly deemed slow either. What the ship lacked in speed, it made up for with size, luxury and supposedly safety.

◀ The Titanic Gym had all the latest equipment of the day.

▶ A gold pocket watch belonging to passenger and victim Thomas Brown was found and returned to his wife who survived when she was 91 years old.

◀ A silver filigree pendant was recovered with all 68 gemstones intact.

◀ The lavish first class smoking room was popular with the wealthy travelers.

◀ The barber shop also sold souvenirs to first class passengers.

▶ The first class lounge on both the Titanic and th Olympic were decorated like the palace of Versailles.

THE INTERIOR OF THE TITANIC WAS UNLIKE ANYTHING EVER SEEN BEFORE ON A LUXURY CRUISE LINER. THE DECORATION WOULD STILL RATE WITH ANY FIVE STAR HOTEL TODAY.

Never before had an Ocean Liner displayed such luxury as the RMS Titanic. From the lavish suites for First Class passengers to the comfortable rooms for Third Class travelers, Titanic was a sight to behold. Highlighted by a grand staircase with a glass dome, oil paintings, statues and architecture engraved in the walls, the concept of luxurious travel across the Atlantic was transformed by this remarkable ocean liner. Other features included a Turkish steam bath, the first swimming pool ever on an Ocean liner, a Squash court and first class restaurants. Gold plated light fixtures illuminated the first class dining saloon, which was over 100 feet in length. The first class staterooms were suites for the wealthy travelers that included sitting rooms, two bedrooms, wardrobe rooms, a private bath and lavatory.

Public rooms included the Verandah Cafe, a reading and writing room, an outdoor sidewalk Cafe and a gymnasium with stationary bikes and rowing machines. Even in 1912 the Titanic had all the makings of what a modern day hotel would feature today. It was said that traveling in second class on the Titanic would be like going first class on another ship. Third class or steerage passengers were treated to accommodations usually reserved for second class travelers. In years before the Titanic the term 'steerage' was used because both people and cattle could legally be transported in the same quarters. By 1912 this term had become obsolete but was occasionally used as a term to demean the lower class travelers. On Titanic however, Third Class passengers mostly were traveling in conditions that exceeded their own living situation.

◀ People wave goodbye as the ship leaves from the dock.

Passengers ▶ wait to board Titanic in Queenstown.

◀ A silver plated razor and a box with steel razor blades were retrieved from the sunken ship.

◀ Second class riders head on board in Ireland.

▲ A view of the Titanic above the dock at Southampton.

▼ A shot of passengers crowding the gangway along with news photographers.

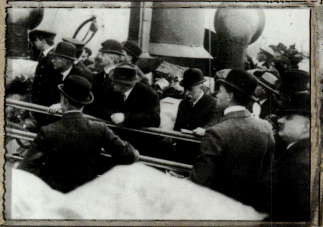

Il y avait beaucoup de personnalités honorables associées avec le légendaire TITANIC. Depuis ses constructeurs jusqu'à son équipe, le TITANIC avait tout de son côté sauf le Destin.

THERE WERE MANY HONORABLE INDIVIDUALS ASSOCIATED WITH THE LEGENDARY TITANIC. FROM ITS BUILDERS TO ITS CREW THE TITANIC HAD EVERYTHING ON ITS SIDE EXCEPT FOR FATE.

Along with the legend of the ship itself, many notable individuals attained folk hero status as a result of their part in the Titanic building and voyage. J. Pierpont Morgan owned the White Star Line Company that hired the crew and operated the ships. Bruce Ismay was the White Star Chairman of the line and a surviving passenger as well. Lord James Prince was in charge of building the ship for the Harland & Wolff company. Alexander Carlisle was the featured designer of the ship for Harland and Wolff. Captain Edward John Smith was the experienced leader of Titanic's maiden voyage. He perished with the ship in its final moments. Captain Arthur Rostron helped recover the lifeboat survivors with his boat the Carpathia. Other notables include Wallace Hartley, a band leader who led a group of eight musicians in a performance until just moments before the ship went down. Fredrick Fleet was the man in the crow's nest who first spotted the iceberg. The Unsinkable Molly Brown led several women into lifeboats before taking charge on lifeboat number six. Colonel Archibald Gracie was a survivor who wrote a well-regarded account of the disaster. Sadly however, he died before its publication. First Officer William Murdoch also perished with Titanic, although his death has become a subject of controversy. Rumors existed that the 39 year old officer took his own life by shooting himself just before the boat went down. Second Officer Lightoller swore that his friend Murdoch would never have committed such an act and claims that he was on the main deck when the boat split in half and went down. Either way, his body was not one of those recovered, hence leaving this mystery unsolved.

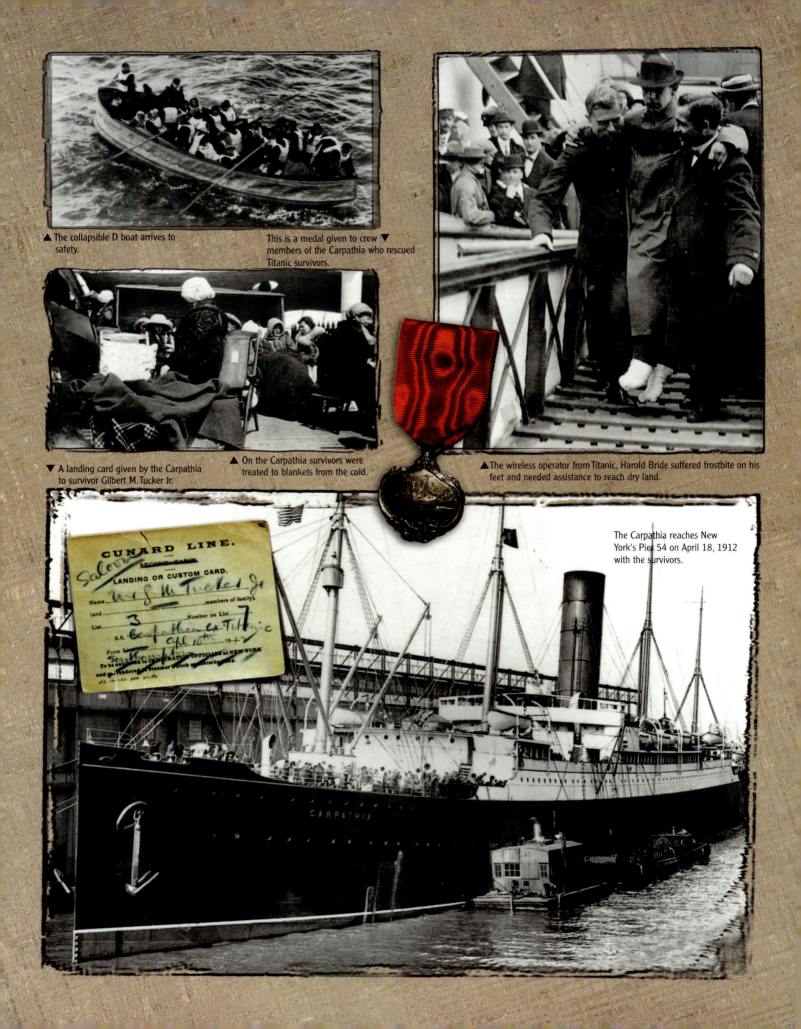

▲ The collapsible D boat arrives to safety.

This is a medal given to crew members of the Carpathia who rescued Titanic survivors. ▼

▼ A landing card given by the Carpathia to survivor Gilbert M. Tucker Jr.

▲ On the Carpathia survivors were treated to blankets from the cold.

▲ The wireless operator from Titanic, Harold Bride suffered frostbite on his feet and needed assistance to reach dry land.

The Carpathia reaches New York's Pier 54 on April 18, 1912 with the survivors.

Dans les eaux glacées de l'Atlantique, beaucoup des passagers du TITANIC furent sauvés grâce aux canots-de-sauvetage. Malheureusement, il n'y en avait pas assez à-bord pour tous les Voyageurs...

IN THE FREEZING WATERS OF THE ATLANTIC MANY PASSENGERS OF THE TITANIC WERE RESCUED BY LIFEBOATS. UNFORTUNATELY THERE WERE NOT NEARLY ENOUGH FOR ALL ON BOARD.

With the temperature only 31 degrees, the waters of the Atlantic were nearly frozen and hardly a place of refuge for the passengers of Titanic. Those people who did not manage to escape in lifeboats were simply doomed. After only minutes in the freezing cold water, the average person is subject to frostbite, hypothermia, gangrene, cardiac arrest and instant death. By the time the rescue boats reached the site of the sunken ship, there were only floating bodies to collect. Just 705 people survived on the lifeboats provided. Many who stayed on board until the final moments were hanging on to false hope that a mystery ship in the distance would come to rescue them. The ship in question was called the Californian, but it apparently did not see the flares shot off by the Titanic as the crew had turned in for the night. Captain Smith was one who seemed to think that the boat on the horizon could be his savior. However, just minutes before the ship went under, he thanked his crew and released them of their duty, telling each one to try and save themselves. When 12 crew members grabbed onto an overturned raft in the Ocean, some claimed to have seen Captain Smith swimming towards them for safety. However, when he was told that even one more man would tip the inflatable over, he wished them good luck and swam off in another direction until he froze still in the water. His body was not recovered. One rumor also had Captain Smith saving the life of an infant child by delivering it to the inflatable raft before swimming away. However, no children of any age were rescued from the raft and none of the survivors gave such an account during the investigation into the tragedy.

▲ A memorial service is held on April 22, 1912 in Queenstown.

▶ Robert Ismay is questioned by the American Senators investigation.

▼ 13,000 feet below the Atlantic rests the intact bow of the Titanic.

▶ A compass from Titanic was also recovered with the debris.

▼ Opening statements are held in Scotland for the formal investigation on the sinking of Titanic.

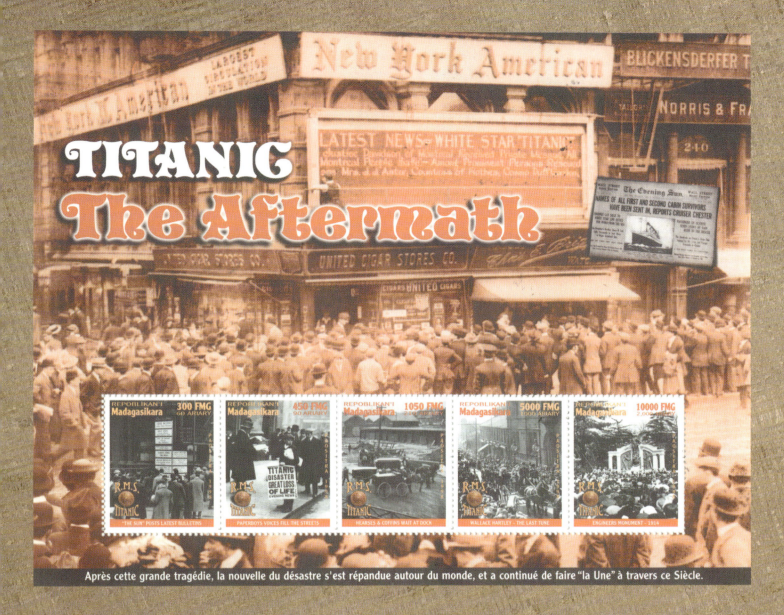

Après cette grande tragédie, la nouvelle du désastre s'est répandue autour du monde, et a continué de faire "la Une" à travers ce Siècle.

FOLLOWING THE GREAT TRAGEDY WORD OF THE DISASTER SPREAD AROUND THE WORLD AND HAS CONTINUED TO MAKE HEADLINES THROUGHOUT THE CENTURY.

The news of the Titanic's sinking did not spread as quickly as it would today. Due to limited communications in 1912, many facts came in slowly causing even the most reputable publications to make errors with the facts. Not until days after the surviving passengers returned did the media learn of who survived and who perished. At first it was even reported by some outlets that the ship was damaged and being towed into Canada. Later the number of casualties was underestimated. Even today the exact number of passengers is not known to a man. White Star hired several ships to recover the bodies from the wreck. One boat, the McKay-Bennett found 306 victims but 116 of them were buried at sea. Only those bodies that were identifiable or in good condition were kept for burial. It was determined by medical examiners that most victims died of exposure to the cold, not drowning as some would assume.

The recovered bodies were laid to rest in three different cemeteries in Halifax, Nova Scotia. Several memorial services were held in Halifax, NY and England to remember the victims of the Titanic. For more than a month following the tragedy, Newspapers were filled with stories about survivors, the inquiries on both sides of the Atlantic and the memorial services. Of all the newspaper accounts that followed the sinking of Titanic, none was more poignant than the words expressed by survivor Dr. Washington Dodge to the San Francisco Bulletin on April 19, 1912. In discussing his view from the lifeboat which carried he and his family Dr. Dodge said "I will never forget the awful scene of the great steamer as we drew away. From the upper rails heroic husbands and fathers were waving and throwing kisses to their womenfolk in the receding lifeboats." And he was one of the lucky ones.

100 NOTABLE FACTS ABOUT TITANIC

1. The port of registry for Titanic was Liverpool, England
2. The ship was named officially in Southampton, UK, although it was built in Belfast.
3. According to estimates the ship would cost approximately $400 million to be rebuilt today.
4. The ship's build number was 401
5. The radio signal call for the Titanic was MGY.
6. In New York City the arrival pier for the ill-fated voyage was Pier 59.
7. The lowest individual ticket price from England to NY was $36.25 on the Titanic. A First Class Suite went for about $4,000 which is today equivalent to $50,000.
8. It cost a nominal fee of $1 to use the Turkish bath on Titanic.
9. The swimming pool on the Titanic was the first ever on an ocean liner.
10. The Titanic was actually larger than its sister ship the Olympic.
11. The Titanic had three propellers.
12. More than 3 million rivets were used to build the luxury liner.
13. The ship was equipped with three electric elevators for passengers to use.
14. The Titanic had 12 watertight doors making it seem unsinkable. It took about 30 seconds for these electrical doors to close.
15. Two barber shops were found on the ship. One in first class and one in second class.
16. The Titanic carried 40,000 eggs, 80,000 pounds of potatoes and 36,000 oranges.
17. According to records, the Titanic launch took 62 seconds in Belfast.
18. Horsepower for the boat was nearly 51,000 and the ship carried 6,307 tons of coal for fuel.
19. The Titanic's anchors weighed 31 tons.
20. There were 18 compasses on the Titanic.
21. On the night the boat sank, Capt. Edward Smith was the guest of honor at a dinner party organized by several prominent passengers. He did not drink wine or liquor at the dinner party. The Dinner party was held in the ship's elegant A La Carte Restaurant.
22. Many of the recovered items from the Titanic included silverware and glasses from the restaurant.
23. All glasses, forks, knives and spoons on board contained the White Star Line logo. The Ship carried 12,000 glasses, 26,500 plates, 19,000 spoons and 2,000 salt shakers.
24. The Titanic sailed 386 miles on the first day, 519 on day two and 549 on day three.
25. On the fateful night, the lights in all public areas were shut down at 10:00PM to encourage passengers to turn in for the evening.
26. Only the first class smoking room remained full of people when the collision occurred just before midnight.
27. The time between the sighting of the iceberg and the collision was less than a minute.
28. The Iceberg was spotted by lookout man Frederick Fleet. According to the ship's log, the collision occurred at 11:40PM.
29. Titanic was the very first ship to use the SOS distress signal.
30. Captain Edward Smith was not on the boat's bridge during the collision.
31. In 1914 an International Ice Patrol was formed to avert any future iceberg incidents.
32. Only 10% of an iceberg is actually visible above water, while the rest is below the water's surface.
33. An iceberg was photographed the following day with a streak of red paint that is believed to be the one that sunk the Titanic.
34. The crew and passengers were mostly fooled by the slightness of the impact.
35. The Titanic passengers had

not been given a lifeboat drill before the collision.
36. Due to the cold weather, many passengers had to scramble to put on warm clothing and life jackets.
37. It was just 31 degrees outside during the time the boat sank. The water was well below the freezing point.
38. The evacuation began 45 minutes after the collision occurred.
39. It was a full hour after the collision when Capt. Smith ordered the distress rockets to be fired.
40. Eight musicians led by violinist Wallace Hartley played songs on the deck while the ship sank. They were traveling as Second Class passengers.
41. The band took requests from the passengers from the White Star Songbook to calm the worried crowd.
42. It is believed by survivors that the band played until the very final moments before the ship went under. The final song played was said to be a hymn entitled Nearer My God To Thee. All eight musicians on Titanic did not survive.
43. American Singer/songwriter Harry Chapin immortalized the musicians with his 1970's song Dance Band on the Titanic.
44. Karl Behr, a Top Ten US Tennis Player was one of the survivors.
45. Macy's Department Store Founder Isidor Strauss and his wife Ida both perished with Titanic.
46. John Jacob Astor, the wealthiest passenger did not survive, but his wife managed to escape safely. Astor's body was recovered with more than $2,500 in his pocket.
47. Fifty five people cancelled their trip on Titanic before it's maiden voyage.
48. All members of the engineering staff were lost with the ship.
49. It took a full two hours and forty minutes for the boat to sink. It was thought by the crewmen that it would take 8 hours for the boat to sink.
50. Brave crewmen kept the lights on for the entire ship until moments before it broke apart.
51. The lifeboats were kept on hinged wood chocks on the boat deck. There were only 20 lifeboats on the ship.
52. Titanic's own Chief Officer Henry Wilde apparently did have some doubt about the ship. He sent a letter to his sister from Queenstown which read, "I still don't like this ship... I have a queer feeling about it." He did not survive.
53. Many of the lifeboats were sent out at less than full capacity.
54. Out of a lifeboat capacity for 1,178 persons, only 705 survived. . One lifeboat left with only 12 people on board out of a possible 65 seats.
55. The lifeboats had the inscription SS Titanic on them, even though the boat was called the RMS Titanic.
56. In addition to the 705 survivors of the ship two pet

This second class luggage tag indicates the Southampton-New York route of Titanic's maiden voyage.

A £5 note from the Bank of England, and a $5 bill from the California National Bank.

Facing page, top to bottom;

Flares are fired from Titanic in a desperate attempt to call the attention of other ships.

A deck of cards belonging to Howard Irwin was carefully separated and cleaned by expert paper restorers in Burgundy, France.

Decorative China dishes for first class passengers.

White Star Line's logo was emblazoned on many items including this cut crystal carafe.

First class passengers, were served with this chocolate pot and vermeil sauce boat, retrieved from the wreck site in 1987.

This second class luggage tag indicates the Southampton–New York route of Titanic's maiden voyage.

A £5 note from the Bank of England, and a $5 bill from the California National Bank.

First class passengers, were served with this chocolate pot and vermeil sauce boat, retrieved from the wreck site in 1987.

Facing page, top to bottom:

Flares are fired from Titanic in a desperate attempt to call the attention of other ships.

A deck of cards belonging to Howard Irwin was carefully separated and cleaned by expert paper restorers in Burgundy, France.

Decorative China dishes for first class passengers.

White Star Line's logo was emblazoned on many items including this cut crystal carafe.